Customs and

from

Cornish Folklore

Robert Hunt

Tor Mark Press · Penryn

First published 1991 by Tor Mark Press,
Islington Wharf, Penryn, Cornwall TR10 8AT
© 1991 Tor Mark Press
ISBN 0-85025-328-4

The cover illustration is by Linda Garland.
Printed in Great Britain by Swannack Brown & Co Ltd, Hull

Introduction

The material for this book is all taken from Robert Hunt's *Popular Romances of the West of England,* published in 1865.

Hunt was the posthumous son of a naval captain and was born in 1807 at Devonport. He went to school in Plymouth and Penzance, then was apprenticed to a surgeon in London. After five years as a physician, he suffered a severe breakdown and resolved to convalesce in the West Country and 'to visit each relic of Old Cornwall and to gather up every existing tale of its ancient people'.

As a child he had visited Bodmin with his mother and heard tales of Hender the huntsman and legends of a devil who had played strange pranks with a tower that stands on a neighbouring hill. The notebook in which he recorded these tales had been lost, and when he returned to recover the tales, the memory of them had gone from the people.

Determined that no further 'drolls and romances' should be lost for ever, for ten months he roamed Cornwall and the borders of Dartmoor, sitting at the hearths of the country people or in close companionship with the miners, 'drinking deep from the stream of legendary lore which was at that time flowing as from a well of living water.' He also met possibly the last two full-time wandering story-tellers left in Cornwall, blind Uncle Anthony James and Billy Frost of St Just.

Thirty years were to pass between this first collection and publication of Hunt's work. In that time he established himself as an important scientific writer and a Fellow of the Royal Society, founded a Mechanics' Institute in Plymouth, became a lecturer and later professor at the Royal School of Mines as well as President of the Cornwall Polytechnic Society, and for 37 years was keeper of mining records for the country. His most important technical work was *British Mining,* a monumental survey published in 1884, three years before his death.

Hunt acknowledged the help he received from many people in his compilation of Cornish folk-lore, including William Bottrell who was to publish his own collection in 1880 in three volumes as *Traditions and Hearthside Stories*.

Further selections from Hunt's work will be found in *Cornish Legends, Cornish Folklore* and *Demons, Ghosts and Spectres in Cornish Folklore,* all published in this series.

Customs

May-day

The first of May is inaugurated with much uproar. As soon as the clock has told of midnight, a loud blast on tin trumpets proclaims the advent of May. This is long continued. At day-break, with their 'tintarrems', they proceed to the country, and strip the sycamore-trees (called May-trees) of all their young branches, to make whistles. With these shrill musical instruments they return home. Young men and women devote May-day to junketing and pic-nics.

It was a custom at Penzance, and probably at many other Cornish towns, when the author was a boy, for a number of young people to sit up until twelve o'clock, and then to march round the town with violins, and fifes, and summon their friends to the Maying.

When all were gathered, they went into the country, and were welcomed at the farmhouses at which they called, with some refreshment in the shape of rum and milk, junket, or something of that sort.

They then gathered the 'May', which included the young branches of any tree in blossom or fresh leaf. The branches of the sycamore were especially cut for the purpose of making the 'May-music'. This was done by cutting a circle through the bark to the wood a few inches from the end of the branch. The bark was wetted and carefully beaten until it was loosened and could be slid off from the wood. The wood was cut angularly at the end, so as to form a mouth-piece, and a slit was made in both the bark and the wood, so that when the bark was replaced a whistle was formed. Prepared with a sufficient number of May whistles, all the party returned to the town, the band playing, whistles blowing, and the young people singing some appropriate song.

Allhallows-Eve at St Ives

The ancient custom of providing children with a large apple on Allhallows-eve is still observed, to a great extent, at St Ives. 'Allan-day', as it is called, is the day of days to hundreds of children, who would deem it a great misfortune were they to go to bed on 'Allan-night' without the time-honoured Allan apple to hide beneath the pillows. A quantity of large apples are thus disposed of, the sale of which is dignified by the term Allan Market.

The Game of Hurling

The game of hurling was, until a recent period, played in the parishes to the west of Penzance on the Sunday afternoon. The game was usually between two parishes, sometimes between Burian and Sancreed, or against St Leven and Sennen, or the higher side of the parish played against the lower side.

The run was from Burian Cross in the Church-town, to the Pipers in Boloeit. All the gentry from the surrounding parishes would meet at Boloeit to see the ball brought in.

Hurling matches are peculiar to Cornwall. They are trials of skill between two parties, consisting of a considerable number of men, forty to sixty a side, and often between two parishes. These exercises have their name from hurling a wooden ball, about three inches in diameter, covered with a plate of silver, which is sometimes gilt, and has commonly a motto, 'Gware wheag yeo gware teag', 'Fair play is good play'. The success depends on catching the ball dexterously when thrown up, or dealt, and carrying it off expeditiously, in spite of all opposition from the adverse party; or, if that be impossible, throwing it into the hands of a partner, who in his turn, exerts his efforts to convey it to his own goal, which is often three or four miles' distance. This sport, therefore, requires a nimble hand, a quick eye, a swift foot, and skill in wrestling; as well as strength, good wind, and lungs. Formerly it was practised annually by those who attended corporate bodies in surveying the bounds of parishes; but from the many accidents that usually attended that game, it is now scarcely ever practised.

Towednack Cuckoo Feast

The parish feast takes place on the nearest Sunday to the 28th of April.

It happened in very early times, when winters extended further into the spring than they now do, that one of the old inhabitants resolved to be jovial, notwithstanding the inclemency of the season; so he invited all his neighbours, and to warm his house he placed on the burning faggots the stump of a tree. It began to blaze, and, inspired by the warmth and light, they began to sing and drink; when, lo! with a whiz and a whir, out flew a bird from the hollow in the stump, crying, Cuckoo! cuckoo! The bird was caught and kept by the farmer, and he and his friends resolved to renew the festal meeting every year at this date, and to call it their 'cuckoo feast'. Previous to this event Towednack had no 'feasten Sunday', which made this parish a singular exception to the rule in Cornwall.

This feast is sometimes called 'crowder' feast, because the fiddler formed a procession at the church door, and led the people through the village to some tune on his 'crowd'.

The Duke of Restormel

A very singular custom formerly prevailed at Lostwithiel, in Cornwall, on Easter Sunday. The freeholders of the town and manor having assembled together, either in person or by their deputies, one among them, each in his turn, gaily attired and gallantly mounted, with a sceptre in his hand, a crown on his head, and a sword borne before him, and respectfully attended by all the rest on horseback, rode through the principal street in solemn state to the church. At the churchyard stile, the curate, or other minister, approached to meet him in reverential pomp, and then conducted him to church to hear divine service. On leaving the church, he repaired, with the same pomp and retinue, to a house previously prepared for his reception. Here a feast, suited to the dignity he had assumed, awaited him and his suite; and, being placed at the head of the table, he was served, kneeling, with all the rites and ceremonies that a real prince might expect. This ceremony ended with the dinner; the prince being voluntarily disrobed, and descending from his momentary exaltation, to mix with common mortals. On the origin of this custom but one opinion can be reasonably entertained, though it may be difficult to trace the precise period of its commencement. It seems to have originated in the actual appearance of the prince, who resided at Restormel Castle in former ages; but, on the removal of royalty, this mimic grandeur stepped forth as its shadowy representative, and continued for many generations as a memorial to posterity of the princely magnificence with which Lostwithiel had formerly been honoured.

This custom is now almost forgotten, and Lostwithiel has little to disturb its quiet.

Geese-Dancing — Plough Monday

The first Monday after Twelfth-day is Plough Monday, and it is the ploughman's holiday.

At this season, in the Islands of Scilly, at St Ives, Penzance, and other places, the young people exercise a sort of gallantry called 'geese-dancing.' The maidens are dressed up for young men, and the young men for maidens; and, thus disguised, they visit their neighbours in companies, where they dance, and make jokes upon what has happened during the year, and every one is humorously 'told their own,' without offence being taken. By this sort of sport, according to yearly custom and toleration, there is a spirit of wit and drollery kept up among the people. The music and dancing done, they are treated with liquor, and then they go to the next house, and carry on the same sport. A correspondent, writing to the *Table-Book* insists on calling these revels 'goose-dancing.' The true Cornishman never uses the term, which is, as I have elsewhere shown, derived from *dance deguisée* — hence guise-dancing, or geese-dancing, by corruption.

Crying the Neck

Owing to the uncertain character of the climate of Cornwall, the farmers have adopted the plan of gathering the sheaves of wheat, as speedily as possible, into 'arish-mows.' These are solid cones from ten to twelve feet high, the heads of the stalks turned inwards, and the whole capped with a sheaf of corn inverted. Whence the term, I know not; but 'arish' is commonly applied to a field of corn recently cut, as, 'Turn the geese in upon the arish' — that is, the short stubble left in the ground.

After the wheat is all cut on most farms in Cornwall and Devon, the harvest people have a custom of 'crying the neck.' I believe that this practice is seldom omitted on any large farm in these counties. It is done in this way. An old man, or some one else well acquainted with the ceremonies

6

used on the occasion (when the labourers are reaping the last field of wheat), goes round to the shocks and sheaves, and picks out a little bundle of all the best ears he can find; this bundle he ties up very neat and trim, and plaits and arranges the straws very tastefully. This is called 'the neck' of wheat, or wheaten-ears. After the field is cut out, and the pitcher once more circulated, the reapers, binders, and the women stand round in a circle. The person with 'the neck' stands in the centre, grasping it with both his hands. He first stoops and holds it near the ground, and all the men forming the ring take off their hats, stooping and holding them with both hands towards the ground. They then all begin at once, in a very prolonged and harmonious tone, to cry, 'The neck!' at the same time slowly raising themselves upright, and elevating their arms and hats above their heads; the person with the neck also raising it on high. This is done three times. They then change their cry to 'We yen! we yen!' which they sound in the same prolonged and slow manner as before, with singular harmony and effect, three times. This last cry is accompanied by the same movements of the body and arms as in crying 'the neck.'

Well, after this they all burst out into a kind of loud, joyous laugh, flinging up their hats and caps into the air, capering about, and perhaps kissing the girls. One of them then gets 'the neck,' and runs as hard as he can down to the farmhouse, where the dairy-maid, or one of the young female domestics, stands at the door prepared with a pail of water. If he who holds 'the neck' can manage to get into the house in any way unseen, or openly by any other way than the door at which the girl stands with the pail of water, then he may lawfully kiss her; but if otherwise, he is regularly soused with the contents of the bucket. I think this practice is beginning to decline of late, and many farmers and their men do not care about keeping up this old custom. The object of crying 'the neck' is to give notice to the surrounding country of the end of the harvest, and the meaning of 'we yen' is 'we have ended.' It may probably mean 'we end,' which the uncouth and provincial pronunciation has corrupted into 'we yen.' The 'neck' is generally hung up in the farmhouse, where it often remains for three or four years.

Midsummer Superstitious Customs

If on midsummer-eve a young woman takes off the shift which she has been wearing, and, having washed it, turns its wrong side out, and hangs it in silence over the back of a chair, near the fire, she will see, about midnight, her future husband, who deliberately turns the garment.

If a young lady will, on midsummer-eve, walk backwards into the garden and gather a rose, she has the means of knowing who is to be her husband. The rose must be cautiously sewn up in a paper bag, and put aside in a dark drawer, there to remain until Christmas-day.

On the morning of the Nativity the bag must be carefully opened in silence, and the rose placed by the lady in her bosom. Thus she must wear it to church. Some young man will either ask for the rose, or take it from her without asking. That young man is destined to become eventually the lady's husband.

The practice of sowing hemp-seed on midsummer-eve is not especially a Cornish superstition, yet it was at one time a favourite practice with young women to try the experiment. Many a strange story have I been told as to the result of the sowing, and many a trick could I tell of, which has been played by young men who had become acquainted with the secret intention of some maidens. I believe there is but little difference in the rude rhyme used on the occasion —

> Hemp-seed I sow,
> Hemp-seed I hoe,

(the action of sowing the seed and of hoeing it in, must be deliberately gone through)

> And he
> Who will my true love be,
> Come after me and mow.

A phantom of the true lover will now appear, and of course the maid or maidens retire in wild affright.

If a young unmarried woman stands at midnight on Midsummer-eve in the porch of the parish church, she will see, passing by in procession, every one who will die in the parish during the year. This is so serious an affair that it is not, I believe, often tried. I have, however, heard of young women who have made the experiment. But every one of the stories relate that, coming last in the procession, they have seen shadows of themselves; that from that day forward they have pined, and ere midsummer has again come round, that they have been laid to rest in the village graveyard.

The Helston 'Furry'

This ancient custom, which consists in dancing through the streets of the town, and entering the houses of rich and poor alike, is thus well described in Hone's *Every Day Book:*
'On the 8th of May, at Helstone, in Cornwall, is held what is called the Furry. The word is supposed by Mr Polwhele to have been derived from the old Cornish word *fer,* a fair or jubilee. The morning is ushered in by the music of drums and kettles, and other accompaniments of a song, a great part of which is inserted in Mr Polwhele's history, where this circumstance is noticed. So strict is the observance of this day as a general holiday, that should any person be found at work, he is instantly seized, set astride on a pole, and hurried on men's shoulders to the river, where he is sentenced to leap over a wide place, which he, of course, fails in attempting, and leaps into the water. A small contribution towards the good cheer of the day easily compounds for the leap. About nine o'clock the revellers appear before the grammar-school, and demand a holiday for the schoolboys, after which they collect contributions from houses. They then *fade* into the country (fade being an old English word for *go*), and, about the middle of the day, return with flowers and oak-branches in their hats and caps. From this time they dance hand in hand through the streets, to the sound of the fiddle, playing a particular tune, running into every house they pass without opposition. In the afternoon a select party of the ladies and gentlemen make a progress through the street, and very late in the evening repair to the ball-room. A stranger visiting the town on the eighth of May would really think the people mad, so apparently wild and thoughtless is the merriment of the day. There is no doubt of the Furry originating from the *Floralia,* anciently observed by the Romans on the fourth of the calends of May.'

The Mayor of Halgaver Moor

The people of Bodmin had an old custom of assembling in large numbers on Halgaver Moor in the month of July, and electing a 'Mayor of Misrule', for the punishment of petty offenders. Our old historian gives a quaint description:

'The youthlyer sort of Bodmin townsmen use sometimes to sport themselves by playing the box with strangers, whom they summon to Halgaver; the name signifieth the Goats' Moore, and such a place it is, lying a little without the town, and very full of quagmires. When these mates meet with any raw serving-man or other young master, who may serve and deserve to make pastime, they cause him to be solemnly arrested for his appearance before the Mayor of Halgaver, where he is charged with wearing one spur, or wanting a girdle, or some such like felony, and after he hath been arraigned and tried with all requisite circumstances, judgment is given in formal terms, and executed in some one ungracious prank or other, more to the scorn than hurt of the party condemned. Hence is sprung the proverb, when we see one slovenly apparelled, to say, "He shall be presented in Halgaver Court".'

Sham Mayor

There was a curious custom in the town of Penryn in Cornwall, which long outlived all modern innovations. On some particular day in September or October, about when the hazel-nuts are ripe, the festival of nutting-day is kept. The rabble of the town go into the country to gather nuts, returning in the evening with boughs of hazel in their hands, shouting and making a great noise. In the meantime the journeymen tailors of the town have proceeded to the adjoining village of Mylor, and elected one of their number 'Mayor of Mylor', taking care the selection falls on the wittiest. Seated in a chair shaded with green boughs, and borne on the shoulders of four stalwart men, the worthy mayor proceeds from his 'good town of Mylor' to his 'ancient borough of Penryn', the van being led by the 'bodyguard' of stout fellows well armed with cudgels (which they do not fail to use should their path be obstructed), torch-bearers, and two 'town serjeants,' clad in official gowns and cocked hats, and carrying each a monstrous cabbage on his shoulder in lieu of a mace. The rear is brought up by the rabble of the 'nutters'. About mid-day a band of music meets them, and plays them to Penryn, where they are received by the entire population. The procession proceeds to the town-hall, in front of which the mayor delivers a speech, declaratory of his intended improvements for the coming year, being generally an excellent sarcastic burlesque on the speeches of parliamentary candidates. The procession then moves on to each public-house door, where the mayor, his council, and officers, are liberally supplied with liquor, and the speech is repeated with variations. They then adjourn to the 'council-chamber', in some public-house, and devote the night to drinking. At night the streets are filled with people bearing torches, throwing fireballs, and discharging rockets; and huge bonfires are kindled on the Green, and Old Wall. The legal mayor once made an effort to put a stop to this saturnalia, but his new-made brother issued prompt orders to his bodyguards, and the *posse comitatus* had to fly.

The popular opinion is, that there is a clause in the borough charter compelling the legitimate mayor to surrender his power to the 'Mayor of Mylor' on the night in question, and to lend the town sergeants' paraphernalia to the gentlemen of the shears.

Baal Fires

It is the immemorial usage in Penzance and the neighbouring towns and villages to kindle bonfires and torches on Midsummer-eve; and on Midsummer-day to hold a fair on Penzance quay, where the country folks assemble from the adjoining parishes in great numbers to make excursions on the water. St Peter's-eve is distinguished by a similar display of bonfires and torches, although the 'quay-fair' on St Peter's-day has been discontinued upwards of forty years.

On these eves a line of tar-barrels, relieved occasionally by large bonfires, is seen in the centre of each of the principal streets in Penzance. On either side of this line young men and women pass up and down swinging round their heads heavy torches made of large pieces of folded canvas steeped in tar, and nailed to the ends of sticks between three and four feet long; the flames of some of these almost equal those of the tar-barrels.

Rows of lighted candles also, when the air is calm, are fixed outside the windows or along the sides of the streets. In St Just and other mining parishes the young miners, mimicking their fathers' employments, bore rows of holes in the rocks, load them with gunpowder, and explode them in rapid succession by trains of the same substance. As the holes are not deep enough to split the rocks, the same little batteries serve for many years. On these nights Mount's Bay has a most animating appearance, although not equal to what was annually witnessed at the beginning of the present [i.e. nineteenth] century, when the whole coast, from the Land's End to the Lizard, wherever a town or village existed, was lighted up with these stationary or moving fires. In the early part of the evening, children may be seen wearing wreaths of flowers — a custom in all probability originating from the ancient use of these ornaments when they danced around the fires. At the close of the fireworks in Penzance, a great number of persons of both sexes, chiefly from the neighbourhood of the quay, used always, until within the last few years, to join hand in hand, forming a long string, and run through the streets, playing 'thread the needle,' heedless of the fireworks showered upon them, and oftentimes leaping over the yet glowing embers. I have on these occasions seen boys following one another, jumping through flames higher than themselves. But whilst this is now done innocently in every sense of the word, we all know that the passing of children through fire was a very common act of idolatry; and the heathen believed that all persons, and all living things, submitted to this ordeal, would be preserved from evil throughout the ensuing year. A similar blessing was supposed to be imparted to their fields by running around them with flaming torches.

Charms of Healing

The Zennor Charmers

Both men and women in this parish possessed this power to a remarkable degree. They could stop blood, however freely it might be flowing. 'Even should a pig be sticked in the very place, if a charmer was present, and *thought* of his charm at the time, the pig would not bleed.' This statement, made by a Zennor man, shows a tolerably large amount of faith in their power. The charmers are very cautious about communicating their charms. A man would not on any account tell his charm to a woman, or a woman communicate hers to a man. People will travel many miles to have themselves or their children charmed for 'wildfires' (erysipelas), ringworms, pains in the limbs or teeth, 'kennels' (ulcerations) on the eyes. A correspondent writes:

'Near this lives a lady charmer, on whom I called. I found her to be a really clever, sensible woman. She was reading a learned treatise on ancient history. She told me there were but three charmers left in the west, one at New Mills, one in Morva, and herself.'

The Twelve-o'clock Stone

Numbers of people would formerly visit a remarkable Logan stone, near Nancledrea, which had been, by supernatural power, impressed with some peculiar sense at midnight. Although it was quite impossible to move this stone during daylight, or indeed by human power at any other time, it would rock like a cradle exactly at midnight. Many a child has been cured of rickets by being placed naked at this hour on the twelve-o'clock stone. If, however, the child was 'misbegotten' or if it was the offspring of dissolute parents, the stone would not move, and consequently no cure was effected. On the Cuckoo Hill, eastward of Nancledrea, there stood, but a few years since, two piles of rock about eight feet apart, and these were united by a large flat stone carefully placed upon them, thus forming a doorway which was, as my informant told me, 'large and high enough to drive a horse and cart through'. It was formerly the custom to march in procession through this 'doorway' in going to the twelve-o'clock stone.

The stone-mason, has however, been busy hereabout;

and every mass of granite, whether rendered notorious by the Giants or holy by the Druids, if found to be of the size required, has been removed.

Sundry Charms

The vicar of a large parish church informs me that a woman came to him some time since for water from the font after a christening; she required it to undo some spell. The vicar states, that all the fonts in the country were formerly locked, to prevent people from stealing the 'holy water,' as they called it.

Cure for colic in Towednack

To stand on one's head for a quarter of an hour.

For a scald or burn

> There came three angels out of the east,
> One brought fire and two brought frost;
> Out fire and in frost,
> In the name of the Father, Son, and Holy Ghost.
> Amen!

Bramble-leaves, or sometimes the leaves of the common dock, wetted with spring water, are employed in this charm, as also in the following one.

Charms for inflammatory diseases

A similar incantation to that practised for a burn is used. Three angels are invoked to come from the east, and this form of words is repeated three times to each one of nine bramble-leaves immersed in spring water, making passes with the leaves from the diseased part.

Charm to stop bleeding

> Christ was born in Bethlehem,
> Baptized in the river Jordan;
> There he digg'd a well,
> And turn'd the water against the hill,
> So shall thy blood stand still.   In the name, etc.

The sleeping foot

This irregularity in the circulation is at once removed by crossing the foot with saliva.

To cure the hiccough

Wet the forefinger of the right hand with spittle, and cross the front of the left shoe or boot three times, repeating the Lord's Prayer backwards.

The cure of boils

The sufferer is to pass nine times against the sun, under a bramble-bush growing at both ends. This is the same as the cure prescribed for rheumatism.

Rickets, or a crick in the back

The holed stone — Men-an-tol — in Lanyon, is commonly called by the peasantry the crick-stone. Through this the sufferer was drawn nine times against the sun — or, if a man, he was to crawl through the hole nine times.

Tea-stalks and smut

Stems of tea floating in that beverage indicate strangers. Flakes of smut hanging loose to the fire-bars do the same thing.

The time of the stranger's arrival may be known by placing the stem on the back of one hand and smacking it with the other; the number of blows given before it is removed indicates the number of days before his arrival.

The flake of carbon is blown upon, and according as it is removed by the first, second, or third blow, so is the time at the end of which the visitor may be expected.

To choose a wife

Ascertain the day of the young woman's birth, and refer to the last chapter of Proverbs. Each verse from the 1st to the 31st is supposed to indicate, either directly or indirectly, the character, and to guide the searcher — the verse corresponding with her age indicating the woman's character.

Five cures for warts

1. The vicar of Bodmin found, not long since, a bottle full of pins laid in a newly-made grave. I have heard of this as an unfailing remedy; each wart was touched with a new pin, and the pin then dropped into the bottle. I am not quite certain that it was necessary that the bottle should be

placed in a newly made grave; in many cases burying it in the earth, and especially at a 'four cross-roads,' was quite sufficient. As the pins rust, the warts decay.

2. A piece of string should be taken, and as many knots tied on it as there are warts on the body; each wart being carefully touched with the knot dedicated to it. The string is then to be buried, and the warts fade away as it decays. A few years since a shipwright in Devonport dockyard professed to cure warts by merely receiving from an indifferent person a knotted string, the knots of which had been tied by the afflicted. What he did with the string I know not.

3. To touch each wart with a pebble, place the pebbles in a bag, and to lose the bag on the way to church, was for many years a very favourite remedy; but the unfortunate person who found the bag received the warts. A lady once told me that she picked up such a bag, when a child, and out of curiosity, and in ignorance, examined the contents. The result was that she had, in a short time, as many warts as there were stones in the bag.

4. Another remedy was to steal a piece of meat from a butcher's stall in the public market, and with this to touch the warts, and bury it. As the meat putrefied the warts decayed.

5. I remember, when quite a child, having a very large 'seedy wart' on one of my fingers. I was taken by a distant relation, an elderly lady, residing in Gwinear, to some old woman, for the purpose of having this wart charmed. I well remember that two charred sticks were taken from the fire on the hearth, and carefully crossed over the fleshy excrescence, while some words were muttered by the charmer. I know not how long it was before the wart disappeared, but certainly, at some time, it did so.

A cure for paralysis

Margery Penwarne, a paralysed woman, about fifty years of age, though from her affliction looking some ten years older, sat in the church porch and presented her out-stretched withered arm and open palm to the congregation as they left the house of God after the morning service.

Penny after penny fell into her hand, though Margery never opened her lips. All appeared to know the purpose, and thirty pennies were speedily collected. Presently the parson came with his family, and then she spoke for the first time, soliciting the priest to change the copper coins into one silver one. This wish was readily acceded to, and the paralytic woman hobbled into the church, and up the aisle to the altar rails. A few words passed between her and the clerk; she was admitted within the rails, and the clerk moved the communion-table from against the wall, that she might walk around it, which she did three times.

'Now,' said Margery, 'with God's blessing, I shall be cured; my blessed bit of silver must be made into a ring' (this was addressed to the clerk, half aside); 'and within three weeks after it is on my finger I shall get the use of my limbs again.'

This charm is common throughout the three western counties for the cure of rheumatism or for any contraction of the limbs.

A cure for rheumatism

Crawl under a bramble which has formed a second root in the ground. Or get a woman who has been delivered of a child feet foremost, to tread the patient.

Cure of toothache

One good man informed me that, though he had no faith in charming, yet this he knew, that he was underground one day, and had the toothache 'awful bad, sure enough; and Uncle John ax'd me, "What's the matter?" says he. "The toothache," says I. "Shall I charm it?" says he. "Ees," says I. "Very well," says he; and off he went to work in the next ditch. Ho! dedn't my tooth ache, Lor' bless ee; a just ded, ye knaw; just as if the charm were tugging my very life out. At last Uncle John comed down to the soller, and sing'd out, "Alloa! how's your tooth in there," says he. "Very bad," says I. "How's a feeling?" says he. "Pulling away like an ould hoss with the skwitches," says I. "Hal drag my jaw off directly," says I. "Ees the charm working?" says he. "Es, a shure enuf," says I. "Es," says he, "al be better d'rectly." "Hope a will," says I. Goodness gracious! dedn't a ache; I believe a did you; then a stopped most to once. "Es better," says I. "I thought so," says he, "and you waan't have un no more for a long time," says he. "Thank ee, Uncle John," says I; "I'll give ee a pint o' beer pay-day," and so I ded; an' I haben't had the toothache ever since. Now, if he dedn't charm un, how ded a stop? and if he dedn't knaw a would be better a long time, how ded he say so? No, nor I haven't had un never since. So that's a plain proof as he knaw'd all about it, waden't a you?'

I nodded assent, convinced it was useless to argue against such reasoning as that.

The convalescent's walk

If an invalid goes out for the first time and makes a circuit, this circuit must be with the sun; if against the sun, there will be a relapse.

Two cures for whooping-cough

1. Gather nine spar stones from a running stream, taking care not to interrupt the free passage of the water in doing so. Then dip a quart of water from the stream, which must be taken in the direction in which the stream runs; by no means must the vessel be dipped against the stream.

Then make the nine stones red hot, and throw them into the quart of water. Bottle the prepared water, and give the afflicted child a wine-glass of this water for nine mornings following. If this will not cure the whooping-cough, nothing else can, says the believer.

2. A female donkey of three years old was taken, and the child was drawn naked nine times over its back and under its belly. Then three spoonfuls of milk were drawn from the teats of the animal, and three hairs cut from the back and three hairs cut from the belly were placed in it, this was to stand for three hours to acquire the proper virtue, and then the child drank it in three doses.

This ceremony was repeated three mornings running, and my informant said the child was always cured. I knew of several children who were treated in this manner in one of the small villages between Penzance and Madron Church town, some twenty or thirty years since. There were some doggerel lines connected with the ceremony, which have escaped my memory, and I have endeavoured, in vain, to find any one remembering them. They were to the effect that, as Christ placed the cross on the ass's back when he rode into Jerusalem, and so rendered the animal holy, if the child touched where Jesus sat, it should cough no more.

Superstitions

Miners' Warnings and Tokens

Amongst the mining population there is a deeply-rooted belief in warnings. The following, related by a very respectable man, formerly a miner, well illustrates this:

'My father, when a lad, worked with a companion (James or Jim, as he was called) in Germo. They lived close by Old Wheal Grey in Breage. One evening, the daughter of the person with whom they lodged came in to her mother, crying, "Billy and Jim ben out theer for more than a hour, and I ben chasin them among the Kilyur banks, and they waan't let me catch them. As fast as I do go to one, they do go to another." "Hould your tongue, child," said the mother; "twas their forenoon core, and they both ben up in bed this hours." "I'm sure I ben chasin them," said the girl. The mother then went up-stairs and awoke the lads, telling them the story. One of them said, "Tis a warning; somethin will happen in un old end, and I shan't go to mine this core." "Nonsense," said the other; "don't let us be so foolish; the child has been playing with some strangers, and it isn't worth while to be spaled for any such foolishness." "I tell you," replied the other, "I won't go." As it was useless for one man to go alone, both remained away. In the course of the night, however, a run took place in the end they were working in, and tens of thousands of kibblefuls came away. Had they been at work, it was scarcely possible for them to have escaped.'

At Wheal Vor it has always been and is now believed that a fatal accident in the mine is presaged by the appearance of a hare or white rabbit in one of the engine-houses. The men solemnly declare that they have chased these appearances till they were hemmed in apparently, without being able to catch them. The white rabbit on one occasion being run into a windbore lying on the ground and, though stopped in, escaped.

In this mine there appears to be a general belief among the men in 'tokens' and supernatural appearances. A few months since, a fine old man reported, on being relieved from his turn as watcher, that during the night he heard a loud sound like the emptying of a cartload of rubbish in front of the account-house, where he was staying. On going out, nothing was to be seen. The poor fellow, considering the strange sound as a 'warning', pined away and died within a few weeks.

Fishermen's Superstitions

How to eat pilchards

It is unlucky to commence eating pilchards, or indeed any kind of fish, from the head downwards. I have often heard persons rebuked for committing such a grievous sin, which is 'sure to turn the heads of the fish away from the coasts.'

The legitimate process — mark this, all fish-eaters — is to eat the fish from the tail towards the head. This brings the fish to our shores, and secures good luck to the fishermen.

Pilchards crying for more

When there is a large catch of fish (pilchards), they are preserved — put in bulk, as the phrase is — by being rubbed with salt, and placed in regular order, one on the other, head and tails alternately, forming regular walls of fish.

The fish often, when so placed, make a squeaking noise; this is called 'crying for more,' and is regarded as a most favourable sign. More fish may soon be expected to be brought to the same cellar.

The noise which is heard is really produced by the bursting of the air-bladders; and when many break together, which, when hundreds of thousands are piled in a mass, is not unusual, the sound is a loud one.

Whistling

To whistle by night is one of the unpardonable sins amongst the fishermen of St Ives. My correspondent says, 'I would no more dare go among a party of fishermen at night whistling a popular air than into a den of untamed tigers.'

No miner will allow of whistling underground. I could never learn from the miners whether they regarded it as unlucky or not. I rather think they feel that whistling indicates thoughtlessness, and they know their labour is one of danger, requiring serious attention.

The drowned 'hailing their names'

The fishermen dread to walk at night near those parts of the shore where there may have been wrecks. The souls of the drowned sailors appear to haunt those spots, and the 'calling of the dead' has frequently been heard. I have been told that, under certain circumstances, especially before the coming of storms, or at certain seasons, but always at night, these callings are common. Many a fisherman has declared he has heard the voices of dead sailors 'hailing their own names.'

The muryan's bank

The ant is called by the peasantry a muryan. Believing that they are the Small People in their state of decay from off the earth, it is deemed most unlucky to destroy a colony of ants. If you place a piece of tin in a bank of muryans at a certain age of the moon, it will be turned into silver.

The Migratory Birds

I find a belief still prevalent amongst the people in the out-lying districts of Cornwall, that such birds as the cuckoo and the swallow remain through the winter in deep caves, cracks in the earth, and in hollow trees; and instances have been cited of these birds having been found in a torpid state in the mines, and in hollow pieces of wood. This belief appears to be of some antiquity, for Carew writes in his *Survey of Cornwall* as follows:

'In the west parts of Cornwall, during the winter season, swallows are found sitting in old deep tynne-works, and holes in the sea cliffes; but touching their lurking-places, Olaus Magnus maketh a far stranger report. For he saith that in the north parts of the world, as summer weareth out, they clap mouth to mouth, wing to wing, and legge to legge, and so, after a sweet singing, fall downe into certain lakes or pools amongst the caves, from whence at the next spring they receive a new resurrection; and he addeth, for proofe thereof, that the fishermen who make holes in the ice, to dig up such fish in their nets as resort thither for breathing, doe sometimes light on these swallows cong-ealled in clods, of a slymie substance, and that, carrying them home to their stoves, the warmth restored them to life and flight.'

A man employed in the granite quarries near Penryn, informed me that he found such a 'slymie substance' in one of the pools in the quarry where he was working, that he took it home, warmth proved it to be a bird, but when it began to move it was seized by the cat, who ran out on the downs and devoured it.

A Test of Innocency

A farmer in Towednack having been robbed of some property of no great value, was resolved nevertheless, to employ a test which he had heard the 'old people' resorted to for the purpose of catching the thief. He invited all his neighbours into his cottage, and when they were assembled, he placed a cock under the brandice (an iron vessel formerly much employed by the peasantry in baking, when this process was carried out on the hearth, the fuel being furze and ferns). Every one was directed to touch the brandice with his, or her, third finger, and say, 'In the name of the Father, Son, and Holy Ghost, speak.' Every one did as they were directed, and no sound came from beneath the brandice. The last person was a woman, who occasionally laboured for the farmer in his fields. She hung back, hoping to pass unobserved amidst the crowd. But her very anxiety made her a suspected person. She was forced forward, and most unwillingly she touched the brandice, when, before she could utter the words prescribed the cock crew. The woman fell faint on the floor, and, when she recovered, she confessed herself to be the thief, restored the stolen property, and became, it is said, 'a changed character from that day.'

The Bonfire Test

A bonfire is formed of faggots of furze, ferns, and the like. Men and maidens by locking hands form a circle, and commence a dance to some wild native song. At length, as the dancers become excited, they pull each other from side to side across the fire. If they succeed in treading out the fire without breaking the chain, none of the party will die during the year. If, however, the ring is broken before the fire is extinguished, 'bad luck to the weak hands,' as my informant said.

The Ash Tree

Weakly children — 'children that wouldn't goode,' or thrive — were sometimes drawn through the cleft ash tree. I have seen the ceremony performed but in one case.

The tree was young, and it was taken by the two forks, bifurcation having taken place, and by force rended longitudinally. The cleft was kept open, and the child, quite naked, was passed head first through the tree nine times. The tree was then closed and carefuly tied together. If the severed parts reunited, the child and the tree recovered together; if the cleft gaped in any part, the operation was certain to prove ineffectual.

I quote another example. A large knife was inserted into the trunk of the young tree, about a foot from the ground, and a vertical rending made for about three feet. Two men then forcibly pulled the parts asunder, and held them so, whilst the mother passed the child through it three times. This 'passing' alone was not considered effective; it was necessary that the child should be washed for three successive mornings in the dew from the leaves of the 'charmed ash.'

Snakes avoid the Ash Tree

It is said that no kind of snake is ever found near the 'ashen-tree,' and that a branch of the ash tree will prevent a snake from coming near a person.

A child who was in the habit of receiving its portion of bread and milk at the cottage door, was found to be in the habit of sharing its food with one of the poisonous adders. The reptile came regularly every morning, and the child, pleased with the beauty of his companion, encouraged the visits. The babe and adder were close friends.

Eventually this became known to the mother, and, finding it to be a matter of difficulty to keep the snake from the child whenever it was left alone — and she was frequently, being a labourer in the fields, compelled to leave her child to shift for itself — she adopted the precaution of binding an 'ashen-twig' about its body.

The adder no longer came near the child; but from that day forward the child pined, and eventually died, as all around said, through grief at having lost the companion by whom it had been fascinated.

To Charm a Snake

When an adder or snake is seen, a circle is to be rapidly drawn around it, and the sign of the cross made within it, while the two first verses of the 68th Psalm are repeated:

'Let God arise, let his enemies be scattered; let them also that hate him flee before him.

'As smoke is driven away, so drive them away; as wax melteth before the fire, so let the wicked perish at the presence of God.'

When a child, I well remember being shown a snake, not yet dead, within a circle of this kind; the gardener who drew my attention to the reptile informing me that he had charmed it in the manner related.

Adders, and the Milpreve

The country people around the Land's End say that in old times no one could live in the low grounds, which were then covered with thickets, and these swarming with adders. Even at a much later period, in the summer-time, it was not safe to venture amongst the furze on the Downs without a *milpreve*. I have never seen a milpreve; but it is described to me as being about the size of a pigeon's egg, and I am told that it is made by the adders when they get together in great numbers.

A friend writes me: 'I was once shown a milpreve; it was nothing more than a beautiful ball of coralline lime-stone, the section of the coral being thought to be entangled young snakes.'

When some old men were streaming the Bottoms up near Partimey, they were often obliged to leave work on account of the number of adders that would get together as if by agreement, and advance upon them. One day one of the tin streamers chanced to leave his pot of milk, uncovered, out of the moor-house, when an adder got into it. The man cut a turf and put over the pot to prevent the reptile from escaping. In a few minutes the tinners saw 'the ugly things crawling and leaping from all quarters towards the pot.' The streamers were obliged to run, and take which way they would, the adders seemed to be coming from every direction, further and further off.

At last 'they formed a heap round the pot as large as a

pook [cock] of hay.' Towards night all the reptiles were quite still; then the man gathered together, around the mass of adders, a great quantity of furze (being summer, there was plenty cut and dry close at hand) and piled it up like sheaves to make a mow, laying a circle of well-dried turf without it. They then fired the turf on every side, and when it was well ignited, they fired the furze. 'Oh, it was a sight to see the adders when they felt the smoke and the flame! they began to boil, as it were, all in a heap, and fell back into the flaming furze; those which leaped through perishing on the brilliant ring of burning peat. Thus were killed thousands upon thousands of adders, and the moors were clear for a long, long period.'

Moon Superstitions

The following superstitions are still prevalent on the north coast of Cornwall:

'The sea-poppy, so much valued for removing all pains in the breast, stomach, and intestines, is good also for disordered lungs, and is so much better here than in other places, that the apothecaries of Cornwall send hither for it; and some people plant them in their gardens in Cornwall, and will not part with them under sixpence a root. A very simple notion they have with regard to this root, which falls not much short of the Druids' superstition in gathering and preparing their selago and samolus. This root, you must know, is accounted very good both as an emetic and cathartic. If, therefore, they design that it shall operate as the former, their constant opinion is that it should be scraped and sliced upwards — that is, beginning from the root, the knife is to ascend towards the leaf; but if it is intended to operate as a cathartic, they must scrape the root downwards. The *senecio* also, or groundsel, they strip upwards for an emetic and downwards for a cathartic. In Cornwall they have several such groundless opinions with regard to plants, and they gather all the medicinal ones when the moon is just such an age; which, with many other such whims, must be considered as the reliques of the Druid superstition.'

They, the Druids, likewise used great ceremonies in gathering an herb called *samolus,* marsh-wort, or fenberries, which consisted in a previous fast, in not looking back during the time of their plucking it, and, lastly, in using their left hand only; from this last ceremony, perhaps, the herb took the name of *samol,* which in the Phoenician tongue means the left hand. The herb was considered to be particularly efficacious in curing the diseases incident to swine and cattle.

Good Luck or Bad Luck

The robin and the wren

> Those who kill a robin or a wran,
> Will never prosper, boy or man.

This feeling is deeply impressed on every young mind; there are few, therefore, who would injure either of those birds. I remember that a boy in Redruth killed a robin: the dead robin was tied round his neck, and he was marched by the other boys through the town, all of them singing the above lines.

Crowing hens, etc

A whistling maid and a crowing hen in one house, is a certain sign of a downfall to some one in it. I have known hens killed for crowing by night.

The braying of an ass is a sign of fair weather; so is also the crowing of a cock. The quacking of ducks foretells rain.

Rain at bridal or burial

> Blessed is the bride
> Whom the sun shines on,
> Blessed is the dead
> Whom the rain rains on.

If it rains while a wedding party are on their way to the church, or on returning from it, it betokens a life of bickering and unhappiness.

If the rain falls on a coffin, it is supposed to indicate that the soul of the departed has 'arrived safe'.

The new moon

To see the new moon for the first time through glass, is unlucky; you may be certain that you will break glass before that moon is out. I have known persons whose attention has been called to a clear new moon hesitate.

'Hev I seed her out a doors afore?' If not, they will go into the open air, and if possible show the moon 'a piece of gold', or, at all events, turn their money.

The spark on the candle

A bright spark on the candle-wick indicates a letter coming to the house. The person towards whom it shines will receive it. The time of its arrival is determined by striking the bottom of the candlestick on the table. If the spark comes off on the first blow, it will be received to-morrow; if two blows are required, on the second day, and so on.

The magpie

> One is a sign of anger,
>> Two is a sign of mirth,
> Three is a sign of a wedding,
>> Four is a sign of a birth [or death]

A scolding woman is called a magpie. Whenever you see a magpie, take off your hat to it; this will turn away the anger.

A loose garter

If an unmarried woman's garter loosens when she is walking, her sweetheart is thinking of her.

The Hand of a Suicide

Placing the hand of a man who has died by his own act is a cure for many diseases. The following is given me by a thinking man, living in one of the towns in the west of Cornwall:

'There is a young man in this town who had been afflicted with running tumours from his birth. When about seventeen years of age he had the hand of a man who had hanged himself, passed over the wounds on his back and, strange to say, he recovered from that time, and is now comparatively robust and hearty. This incident is true; I was present when the charm was performed. It should be observed that the notion appears to be that the "touch" is only effectual on the opposite sex; but in this case they were both, the suicide and the afflicted one, of the same sex.'

This is only a modified form of the superstition that a wen, or any strumous swelling, can be cured by touching it with the dead hand of a man who has just been publicly hanged.

I once saw a young woman led on to the scaffold, in the Old Bailey, for the purpose of having a wen touched with the hand of a man who had just been executed.

The Well at Altar-Nun

Amongst the numerous holy wells which exist in Cornwall, that of Alternon, or Altar-Nun, is the only one, as far as I can learn, which possessed the virtue of curing the insane.

We are told that Saint Nunne or Nuanita was the daughter of an Earl of Cornwall, and the mother of St David; that the holy well which is situated about a mile from the cathedral of St David was dedicated to her; and that she bestowed on the waters of the Cornish well those remarkable powers, which were not given to the Welsh one, from her fondness for the county of her birth.

Carew, in his *Survey of Cornwall,* thus describes the practice:

'The water running from St Nun's well fell into a square and enclosed walled plot, which might be filled at what depth they listed. Upon this wall was the frantic person put to stand, his back towards the pool, and from thence, with a sudden blow in the breast, tumbled headlong into the pond; where a strong fellow, provided for the nonce, took him, and tossed him up and down, alongst and athwart the water, till the patient, by foregoing his strength, had somewhat forgot his fury. Then was he conveyed to the church, and certain masses said over him; upon which handling, if his right wits returned, St Nun had the thanks; but if there appeared small amendment, he was bowssened again and again, while there remained in him any hope of life or recovery.'

The 2nd of March is dedicated to St Nun, and the influence of the water is greatly exalted on that day.

Although St Nun's well has been long famous, and the celebrity of its waters extended far, yet there was a belief prevailing amidst the uneducated, that the sudden shock produced by suddenly plunging an insane person into water was most effective in producing a return to reason.

On one occasion, a woman of weak mind, who was suffering under the influence of a religious monomania, consulted me on the benefit she might hope to receive from electricity. The burden of her ever-melancholy tale was, that 'she had lost her God;' and she told me, with a strange mixture of incoherence and reason, that her conviction was, that a sudden shock would cure her. She had herself proposed to her husband and friends that they should take her to a certain rock on St Michael's Mount, stand her on it, with her back to the sea, when 'the waters were the strongest, at the flowing of the tide;' and after having prayed with her, give her the necessary blow on the chest, and thus plunge her into the waters below. I know not that the experiment was ever made in the case of this poor woman, but I have heard of several instances where this sudden plunge had been tried as a cure for insanity.

The Well of St Keyne

St Keyne came to this well about five hundred years before the Norman Conquest, and imparted a strange virtue to its waters — namely, that whichever of a newly-married couple should first drink thereof, was to enjoy the sweetness of domestic sovereignty ever after.

Situated in a thickly-wooded district, the well of St Keyne presents a singularly picturesque appearance. Four trees grow over the well, imparting a delightful shade, and its clear waters spread an emerald luxuriance around. Once, and once only, have I paid a visit to this sacred spot. Then and there I found a lady drinking of the waters from her thimble, and eagerly contending with her husband that the right to rule was hers. The man, however, mildly insisted upon it that he had had the first drink, as he had rushed before his wife, and dipping his fingers into the water had sucked them. This the lady contended was not drinking, and she, I have no doubt, through life had the best of the argument.

Madron Well

In Madron Well — and, I have no doubt, in many others — may be found frequently the pins which have been dropped by maidens desirous of knowing 'when they were to be married.' I once witnessed the whole ceremony performed by a group of beautiful girls, who had walked on a May morning from Penzance. Two pieces of straw, about an inch long each, were crossed and the pin run through them. This cross was then dropped into the water, and the rising bubbles carefully counted, as they marked the number of years which would pass ere the arrival of the happy day. This practice also prevailed amongst the visitors to the well at the foot of Monacuddle Grove, near St Austell.

On approaching the waters, each visitor is expected to throw in a crooked pin; and, if you are lucky, you may possibly see the other pins rising from the bottom to meet the most recent offering.

Rickety Children

The practice of bathing rickety children on the first three Wednesdays in May is still far from uncommon in the outlying districts of Cornwall. The parents will walk many miles for the purpose of dipping the little sufferers in some well, from which the 'healing virtue' has not entirely departed. Among these holy wells, Cubert is far-famed. To this well the peasantry still resort, firm in the faith that there, at this especial season, some mysterious virtue is communicated to its waters. On these occasions, only a few years since, the crowd assembled was so large, that it assumed the character of a fair.

As it was of old, so is it to-day. It was but yesterday that I stood near the font of Royston Church, and heard the minister read with emphasis, 'None can enter into the kingdom of God except he be regenerate and born anew of water.' Surely the simple faith of the peasant mother who, on a spring morning, takes her weakly infant to some holy well, and three times dipping it in its clear waters, uttering an earnest prayer at each immersion, is but another form of the prescribed faith of the educated church-man.

The Preservation of Holy Wells

It is a very common notion amongst the peasantry that a just retribution overtakes those who wilfully destroy monuments, such as stone circles, crosses, wells, and the like. Mr Blight writes me: 'Whilst at Boscaswell, in St Just, a few weeks since, an old man told me that a person who altered an old Holy Well there, was drowned the next day in sight of his home, and that a person who carried away the stones of an ancient chapel, had his house burned down that very night.' We hope the certainty of punishment will prevent any further spoliation. Cannot we do something towards the preservation of our antiquities?

Some Popular Superstitions

It is, or rather was, believed, in nearly every part of the West of England, that death is retarded, and the dying kept in a state of suffering, by having any lock closed, or any bolt shot, in the dwelling of the dying person.

A man cannot die easy on a bed made of fowls' feathers, or the feathers of wild birds.

Never carry a corpse to church by a new road.

Whenever a guttering candle folds over its cooling grease, it is watched with much anxiety. If it curls upon itself it is said to form the 'handle of a coffin,' and the person towards whom it is directed will be in danger of death.

Bituminous coal not unfrequently swells into bubbles, these bubbles of coal containing carburetted hydrogen gas. When the pressure becomes great they burst, and often throw off the upper section with some explosive force. According to the shape of the piece thrown off, so is it named. If it proves round, it is a purse of money; if oblong, it is a coffin, and the group towards which it flew will be in danger.

If a cock crows at midnight, the angel of death is passing over the house; and if he delays to strike, the delay is only for a short season.

The howling of a dog is a sad sign. If repeated for three nights, the house against which it howled will soon be in mourning.

A raven croaking over a cottage fills its inmates with gloom.

If a corpse stiffens shortly after death, all is thought to proceed naturally; but if the limbs remain flexible, some one of the family is shortly to follow. If the eyes of a corpse are difficult to close, it is said 'they are looking after a follower.'

To find a louse on one's linen, is a sign of sickness. To find two, indicates a severe illness. If three lice are so found within a month, it is a 'token to prepare.'

Talking backwards, or putting one word incorrectly before another — 'the cart before the horse' — is considered to foretell that you will shortly see a stranger.

If two young people, in conversation, happen to think of the same thing at the same time, and one of them utters the thought before the other, that one is certain to be married first.

There are many other superstitions and tokens connected with life and death, but those given show the general character of those feelings which I may, I think, venture to call the 'inner life' of the Cornish people. It will be understood by all who have studied the peculiarities of any Celtic race, that they have ever been a peculiarly impressible people. They have ever observed the phenomena of nature; and they have interpreted them with hopeful feelings, or despondent anxiety, according as they have been surrounded by cheerful or by sorrow-inducing circumstances. That melancholy state of mind, which is so well expressed by the word 'whisht,' leads the sufferer to find a 'sign' or a 'token' in the trembling of a leaf, or in the lowering of the tempest-clouds. A collection of the almost infinite variety of these 'signs and tokens' which still exist, would form a curious subject for an essay. Yet this could only now be done by a person who would skilfully win the confidence of the miner or the peasant. They feel that they might subject themselves to ridicule by an indiscreet disclosure of the religion of their souls. When, if ever, such a collection is made, it will be found that these superstitions have their origin in the purest feelings of the heart — that they are the shadowings forth of love, tinctured with the melancholy dyes of that fear which is born of mystery.

One would desire that even those old superstitions should be preserved. They illustrate a state of society, in the past, which will never again return. There are but few reflecting minds which do not occasionally feel a lingering regret that times should pass away during which life was not a reflection of cold reason.